Edward Hughes, Glyndŵr (1862-1938)

Kevin Mathias

Introduction

In 1895, Edward Hughes, an ambitious young accountant, purchased a fairly large, new, detached red-brick house in Bersham Road, Wrexham at the corner of Princess Street, and moved in with his wife Margaret and their three little daughters. He named the house Glyndŵr, because of a tradition that his family had descended from one of the daughters of Owain Glyndŵr whose palace, Sycharth, lies in Llansilin, where his family had lived for generations.

Edward Hughes was then chief clerk at the Cambrian Leather Works, but already had a number of other business interests and took part enthusiastically in local public life and politics. During the next thirty years it can be said that he became one of the most influential and prominent people in the town. He was a magistrate, borough councillor and later alderman and Freeman of Wrexham, Denbighshire County councillor, landlord and property developer, and joint managing director of the company employing the most workers in the town. He died on Christmas Eve 1938 aged 76. His contribution to the life of the town has now largely been forgotten.

The youngest of his daughters, Edna Winifred, was born in the year before the move to Glyndŵr. She, like her two sisters, lived there for the rest of her life, and died unmarried (as did all three) aged 88, in 1982. She became the custodian of a family archive which had been accumulated over many years and which, by then, quite literally filled the house — apart from the small living area which she occupied. As well as his business and local government interests, her father, in whose shadow they all lived, had been an avid collector of documents and a compiler of local history material, an antiquarian and bibliophile, and the records which were created as a result of all these activities were preserved in this outwardly ordinary house in suburban street. As Miss Edna Hughes neared the end of her life the preservation of the archive became almost her final duty and the one which concerned her most. She finally bequeathed the the Glyndŵr Manuscripts (as they are now called), to the then Clwyd Record Office at Ruthin.

This collection is a record of one remarkable family's contribution to the life of Wrexham, spanning nearly one hundred years.

1. Edward Hughes wearing the regalia of Master of the Square & Compass Lodge, Wrexham, 1912.

Early life

Edward Hughes was born on 12 October 1862 at Upper Brook Street, Oswestry, son of Joseph and Jane Hughes (née Powell). He was the second child in a family of four sons and a daughter. Apart from Edward, none of them lived longer than their early thirties. On his birth certificate Joseph is described as a carrier but in later life became a market inspector. Edward later said that he was the first of his family for centuries not to be born in the parish of Llansilin in the extreme south-east corner of the old Denbighshire. Joseph was the son of Richard Hughes of Votty (or Hafodty). His branch of the family was connected with another at Plas Newydd, also in Llansilin, which had purchased the property from the Myddelton family at the beginning of the nineteenth century. Edward contemplated later, in his then more prosperous circumstances, purchasing the ruinous Plas Newydd, but instead removed an old oak door and a dog gate from the bottom of the collapsed staircase and installed them at Glyndŵr.

The family moved to a farm at Treflach from where Edward attended school at Trefonen and then Oswestry. In November 1877 he was articled to Edward Evans, accountant and coal merchant of Oswestry, receiving three shillings per week for the first six months, five shillings for the second, eight shillings per week for the second year, nine for the third and one pound per week thereafter. When he completed his apprenticeship in 1881 he left to become cashier to Robert Lloyd, draper, in the town. In 1884, at the instigation of his friend W A Bayley, of the family who had founded the *Wrexham Advertiser*, he moved to Wrexham to work as a book-keeper to Jones and Rocke, leather manufacturers. A testimonial given to him by his employer, J Meredith Jones, shows his appreciation of the young accountant: 'Mr Hughes is an excellent penman, quick at accounts, and an accurate book-keeper. As steady as old time, honest as a bishop, and attentive in his duties'. In 1888 when Mr Rocke retired Edward Hughes became chief clerk and head of the office.

In the same year Hughes, then living at 33, Cambridge Terrace, married Margaret Armstrong of Oswestry and moved to 2, Derby Road where two of their three daughters were born. His widowed mother and surviving brothers and sister soon followed him to Wrexham. Edward found brothers John Elias and William Allen employment in the leather works.

Cambrian Leather Works

The works, situated at the junction of Salop Road and Rivulet Road, was the much larger successor on the same site of the sheep-skin tannery founded in 1770 by John Peers. John Smalley, who had earlier been involved as a financial backer to Richard Arkwright, inventor, and who was later to become important in the development of cotton spinning at Holywell in Flintshire, discovered the skins from Peers' tannery to be useful for the rollers and other processes carried out in the manufacture of cotton. On the death of Peers in 1822, Evan Morris became proprietor of the works and in 1858 they were purchased by Messrs James Meredith Jones and Charles Rocke. By the time Edward Hughes joined the company in 1884 the Cambrian Leather Works had a world-wide reputation for roller leather. By 1899 one million sheepskins were being treated annually, to produce not only roller leather but also chamois leather and treated leather for bookbinding and fancy goods. The management of the adjacent Century Tanning Company —which produced leather for belting— was closely related. James Meredith Jones died in 1892 and in 1902 the firm became a limited company with four of his sons as directors and Edward Hughes as Company Secretary. In 1905, two of the sons resigned as directors and were replaced by a new board of management which included Hughes. In 1907 and 1910 the remaining two Jones sons resigned and, on the latter occasion, the former book-keeper was appointed joint managing director with a Charles Prescott, former warehouse manager. His brother William (d. 1908) was assistant manager, and John worked in the company laboratory as assistant chemist to A N Palmer, now much better known for his contribution to local history.

Hughes's records show the meticulous care with which he treated business matters such as reports on the prices of competitors; the requirements of the company's foreign customers in many countries including Russia, India, China and the United States of America; the cost of the forty-five different processes required to produce roller leather (8s 6d per dozen skins); and, with equal consideration, the details of the Cambrian's Sick Benefit Society, football club and fire brigade. In 1910, leather from the works was used to bind the eleventh edition of the *Encyclopaedia Britannica*, a set of which resided in Glyndŵr until Miss Edna Hughes's death. In the same year Edward Hughes's complaint that a mistake had occurred in 'an important telegraphic message' appeared in Hansard when the Member of Parliament, George Osborne Morgan, asked the Postmaster General for his comments on the matter.

In 1922, according to personal memoranda in the Hughes archive, Prescott and others conspired to depose him as managing director and replace him as Company Secretary by Prescott's son.

By 1924 Hughes's position on the board had became untenable and he resigned feeling bitterly resentful.

Hughes later had other business interests, founding the Yale Motor Company of Brook Street selling 'The Wolsely and Morris cars, the Two Best Built Cars in Britain' according to their 1928 brochure. He was a director of the local furniture company, S Aston and Son, secretary to the Wrexham Steam Laundry, and a manager of the Savings Bank. He also collected the prospectuses of many other local companies such as the Wrexham Pavilion and Ice Rink Company (1907) and the Wrexham & District Electric Supply Co Ltd (1891), which he added to the growing archive at Glyndŵr.

Local Government

Edward Hughes was elected to Wrexham Borough Council in 1898. At the time of his death in 1938, he was the 'Father of the Council', its senior Alderman, and had been given the Freedom of the Borough in 1931. After a period of ill health, he had recently tendered his resignation, citing his inability to attend meetings, but the Council had refused to accept it, hoping that he would soon recover and join them once again in the council chamber. He had served on various committees, but his name was connected especially with two of them. As Chairman of the Finance Committee during the period 1908-19 he thoroughly re-organised the Treasurer's Department. It was during this period that the first printed financial statements were made available. Described in his obituary in the *Wrexham Advertiser & Star* as 'a watchdog of finance', it was rumoured that he was accustomed to positioning himself outside the Council Offices to monitor the comings and goings of the staff for the sake of the Borough's economy. Also according to the *Advertiser* he invariably opposed increases at the annual budget meeting of the Council, in the interests of the business community and usually 'died in the last ditch' being the only member to vote against the rate. From 1919 until his death he was the chairman of the Borough Electricity Committee, and member of the North Wales and South Cheshire Joint Electricity Authority, a period which saw the provision of electricity for the Borough set on a firm technical and financial footing.

He was mayor for two successive terms, 1906-7 and 1907-8, which covered the period of the council's celebration of the fiftieth anniversary of its incorporation in 1857. As one would expect, he kept scrapbooks of all the invitations, orders of service and programmes he received during this time and entered into the historical research for the celebrations with enthusiasm, compiling a photographic album with biographical details of all his mayoral predecessors. The sources which he accumulated on the Council's history, it is said, enabled his youngest daughter fifty years later to write the chapter on the early history of Wrexham Borough Council for A H Dodd's (ed.) *A History of Wrexham* from the original documents without having to leave her home.

A feeling for the reputation of Edward Hughes as a member of the Borough Council can be gained again from the *Advertiser*:

> For more than forty years of peace and war he served the town faithfully, and in its service was unsparing of his gifts of shrewdness, foresight and organising ability. His uncompromising adherence to his ideals won for him the respect of those who did not always share his views.

Edward Hughes and politics

As a managing director of the Cambrian Leather Works, Hughes also became influential politically. Press reports described the works as a 'cockpit at election times ... whichever side secures the majority at these works wins'. He was a member of the executive of the Liberal Party in both East Denbighshire and Denbigh Boroughs constituencies, and chairman of the organising committee of the East Denbighshire Liberal Association. The whole family took an interest in political matters, with the children compiling scrap-books, and adding election addresses and even rosettes to the archive. Lloyd George was a visitor to Glyndŵr on more than one occasion, and a leather-backed sheepskin rug which had been used to keep the statesman warm whilst he was being chauffeured somewhere by Edward Hughes was proudly displayed at the house many years later.

Hughes played a crucial political role especially in the first two decades of the twentieth century, a period when the strength of the Labour Party in the area was beginning to assert itself. In the General Election of January 1910 he carried through a Liberal victory with an increased majority largely in the absence of the candidate, E G Hemmerde, who only re-appeared in the constituency three days before the poll. The following December he prevented a split in the Liberal vote and the possible intervention of a Labour candidate by securing the adoption and election of E T John, having also tried to enlist W G C Gladstone, the former Prime Minister's grandson from Hawarden Castle. Hughes himself was rumoured to be considering standing. He had been greatly involved with the brilliant but erratic Hemmerde, the East Denbighshire MP since 1906. Hemmerde, also Recorder of Liverpool, did not stand in the December 1910 election, preferring to fight a seat in Portsmouth, and eventually joined the Labour

Party. His motives and the reaction of Hughes and others can be discovered in the lengthy correspondence preserved in the Glyndŵr archive.

The 1920s saw Hughes trying to unite Liberal and Conservative energies to try to keep Labour out in the Wrexham area, a practically impossible task since the election of 1922. The family, however, always retained their interest in politics and local affairs, and Miss Edna Hughes tried unsuccessfully, on more then one occasion, to be elcted to the Borough Council. She was also an inveterate contributor to the correspondence column of the *Daily Post*, usually on the theme of local government inefficiency and waste.

Public Life

Being one of the area's most prominent citizens brought with it other responsibilities. During the First World War Hughes served as Quartermaster to the Denbighshire Volunteer Regiment with the rank of lieutenant. This was apparently the cause of much amusement to his wife and daughters who considered him helpless when it came to domestic matters. In fact, when he was too busy with business to take holidays at Colwyn Bay with them, he would stay in Wrexham's *Imperial Hotel* until they returned. Nevertheless, Hughes tackled his wartime post with his usual thoroughness and the memoranda, messing accounts, forms, notes and even badges which he retained would almost enable one to set up camp today and feed, clothe and register a large body of men by following his instructions.

As a Welsh speaker, he was in great demand during military recruiting marches throughout north Wales, swearing in the volunteers in their native tongue. He was also a member of the Appeal Tribunal for Denbighshire under the Military Service Act of 1916, and a letter in the archive from Lord Kitchener thanks him for his work and states, 'I shall be glad to hear of any reasons that may be given you by young and suitable men for not availing themselves of this opportunity to see service in the Field where they are so much wanted'. He was also a member of the Food Control, Savings and Pensions Committees. Hughes was awarded an MBE for his war work.

As Mayor, and as a private individual, he was active in many charitable causes, particularly with the NSPCC when his children were young. However, as well as many animal welfare charities, somewhat more surprisingly, the family were supporters of the Discharged Prisoners Aid Society. As a prominent mason, these meetings and events were a constant feature of his diary and he achieved high office, including serving as Master of two Lodges.

Family Life

Edward Hughes must have been an extremely orderly and prudent man. The stocks of stationery which he laid in for his use outlasted him and the rest of his family. The files in his study filing-cabinet were neatly labelled and catalogued, and he would often keep his notes and a draft as well as a copy of a document. One could say that his concern with detail and record-keeping bordered on the fanatical, as with this neatly typed note pasted on a light bulb sleeve '… this lamp was fixed over my desk this date at 12 o'clock noon, 17 September 1936', and also neatly filed away was 'a cutting of felt on roof of the motor house at Frydlyn, Llansilin [his country house], 1928'. Press-cuttings were kept when the value of local people's estates appeared in the local press after their wills were made public, and these were pasted on card and filed. This was also the method which he used for keeping available, in alphabetical order, 'handy' pieces of information ranging from 'A' for anthracite stove ('fixed 21 December 1920, lit about 4 pm — 1 cwt of anthracite nuts from Lager Beer Co lasted until 27 December burning night and day'), to 'W' — 'the world — size of it'.

However, local history was Edward Hughes's main hobby, although one is afraid to use such a word for a pursuit followed with such energy and diligence. He was a frequent contributor to newspapers on the subject, made an historical survey of the houses in his native parish of Llansilin, and transcribed its parish registers as well as those of its neighbouring communities. He was a great friend and supporter of the historian A N Palmer, some of whose working papers, files and notes were added to the Hughes archive after Palmer's death. Hughes's own notes are extensive, and genealogists today should be grateful for his research, including the notes he made of his interviews with old people about their forbears. Although records were the family's chief object, Hughes's antiquarian interests led him to rescue other, larger pieces of Wrexham's heritage, such as the carved beams from the old *Hand Inn* as it was being demolished, not to mention curiosities such as a 'portion of German Zepp brought down in Essex'.

Hughes's records consciousness must have infected his wife Margaret, whose household accounts with local tradesmen have survived in varying degrees of completeness from the beginning of her married life in 1888 until her death in 1947. Observations on the weather were recorded as was the mileage and fuel consumption of their Flanders and Sunbeam cars. The daughters,

2. Miss Edna Hughes, Edward's last surviving daughter, who left the Glyndŵr Collection to the Clwyd Record Office at Ruthin.

Gwendoline, Dorothy and Edna were similarly indoctrinated and practically everything that came into the house, circulars, advertising material, reports and programmes eventually found their way, not always very methodically, into the archive. By this method one gains a fascinating insight into a middle-class family over two generations. Family photographic albums contain snapshots which record amongst other things, long periods of time in their second home at Llansilin, and their great fondness for dogs. Family letters rarely end without 'lots of tail wags, Tiny' or other such canine greeetings.

The family owned property both in Wrexham and Llansilin. Hughes's most prestigious purchase was Croesnewydd Hall, now the centre of Wrexham's Technology Park, and attempted to capitalize on its convenient location by developing it as an industrial site. Having failed, he must have gained some satiasfaction by selling it to Lord Howard de Walden, a descendant of the Myddeltons, to whom it had once belonged.

The impression given of Edward Hughes in public life is of a somewhat ruthless and determined individual, but his many social commitments show that in private he had a more sociable side, for example his outings with the Wrexham Peripatetics, attendance at Masonic functions and charitable and sporting events. Although Edward was undoubtedly head of the household, forbidding, it was said, he gave his daughter Edna a university education, and, from the evidence of their letters, they were a very affectionate and close family enjoying a relatively privileged and comfortable life at Glyndŵr as a result of his success as a businessman.

Note

The publication of this book coincides with the opening of an exhibition of the Glyndŵr Collection at Wrexham County Borough Museum in October 1998. While the exhibition displays all aspects of the collection held by the Denbighshire Record Office at Ruthin, this book serves to provide only a brief selection of the more visual material available.While many of the photographs in the collection have appeared in print elsewhere, there are many pictures that are unique and it is mainly these that are included in this book.

All individuals in group photographs are identified from left to right unless otherwise indicated.

The spelling of Royal Welsh (rather than Welch) Fusiliers follows the convention of the time.

3. (Left) Charles James Apperley

Apperley was a noted writer on country sports using the pen name 'Nimrod' [the Mighty Hunter]. Born at Plas Grono in 1778, he was educated at Rugby School. During the Irish Rebellion of 1799 he served as a cornet (2nd Lieutenant) in the Ancient British Fencible Cavalry. Among his published works are *My Life and Times, Memoirs of the Life of John Mytton, Nimrod Abroad, Nimrod's Sporting Tours*. He died in London in 1843.

4. (Above) Plas Grono, Wrexham

This house was once known as Tŷ Cerig yn Hafod-y-bwch and Plas Newydd. The property of the Yale family, it stood in the grounds of Erddig. In the late 17th century it was the home of Elihu Yale, benefactor of the university in New England which bears his name. In 1731 it was bought by Mr John Mellor of Erddig and was, for a time, the home of the Apperley family (see photograph 3 above). The house was demolished in 1876.

5. (Below) Wrexham & North Wales Bank, 1844.

This bank was founded by Richard Lloyd, a Wrexham mercer and flannel merchant, c1785. With premises in Chester Street, it survived until January 1849 when it failed with liabilities of £48,000. The stamp duty payable on this £5 note was 1/3d (7p).

6. Evan Morris

Evan Morris, a native of Montgomeryshire, came to Wrexham in 1822 and was the proprietor of the leather works which developed into the Cambrian Leather Works. He was the grandfather of Sir Evan Morris, Mayor of Wrexham (see photograph 20). He died in 1859.

7. (Below) Evan Morris & Co Leather Works, 1845.

The works specialised in the production of soft leather for use in industrial rollers, aprons and riding tack. The premises were located between Caia Road and Rivulet Road.

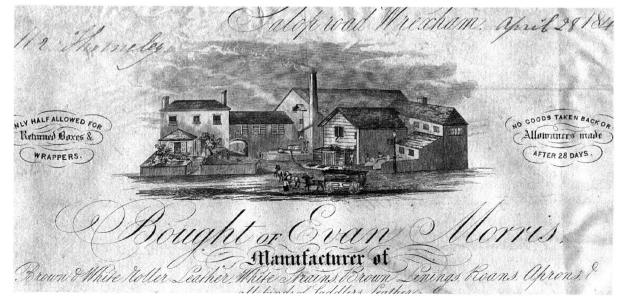

8. Theatre Bill, 1856

A poster advertising the play *Maniac of Chirk Castle* which was performed at the Beast Market Theatre (built by Thomas Penson in the early 19th century). During the time that the theatre was under the management of Mr J Latimer it carried the rather grand title Theatre Royal (as did his other theatres at Stafford, Lichfield, Shrewsbury and Stourbridge). The theatre was eventually demolished to make way for the Eagles Meadow fly-over.

9. (Above) J Meredith Jones

Proprietor of the Cambrian Leather Works. Meredith Jones was against to the incorporation of the Borough and had, some six years earlier, organised a petition to Parliament opposing the Wrexham Improvement Bill and the Public Health Act. When the Charter of Incorporation was granted, Meredith Jones stood for election and came 11th (with 260 votes) in a poll of 52 candidates —the first twelve forming the first Town Council.

10. Thomas Edgeworth

The first Mayor of Wrexham, 1857 and 1858, of Gatefield and Brynygrog. He was a solicitor with offices in Temple Row, Clerk to the Poor Law Guardians and founder of the Wrexham Market Hall Company. Of the candidates for election to the first Council in 1857, Edgeworth came top of the poll with 371 votes and, consequently was chosen as the Borough's first mayor. He died in 1868.

11. (Left) Thomas Painter

The second Mayor of Wrexham (1859). He was the second son of Mr John Painter, printer and bookseller of High Street and was the brother-in-law of William Overton (Mayor 1865). Thomas Painter followed his father into the book business and was, for a time, employed by the London publisher Routledge before setting himself up in various businesses in Wrexham, including lead mining at Minera. In partnership with William Overton he bought the Town Hall in 1857 from where he ran a business as a wine merchant. He died in 1889.

12. (Left) Sergeant-at-Mace
David Higgins, the Borough's first Chief Public Health Inspector, is shown here in the somewhat archaic uniform of Sergeant-at-Mace.

13. (Right) William Turner
He served as Borough Surveyor of Wrexham from 1866-72.

14. (Right) John Dickenson
A native of Cheshire, he was a noted surgeon, residing at Crescent House, Beast Market, Wrexham. In 1847 he is believed to have carried out the first operation using anesthetics in Wales, only some four months after the procedure was introduced in Boston, USA. He was elected to the Borough Council in 1860 and was Mayor in 1861. He died in 1887. His nephew, Dr H V Palin was Mayor in 1889 and 1890.

15. Great Western Railway Station, Spring, 1869

The original railway station designed by Thomas Mainwaring Penson for the Shrewsbury & Chester Railway. Built on the site of the present-day Wrexham General Station, it was demolished in 1881. The Mold Road bridge can be seen on the right. On the platform are: Thomas Knight (Signal Man), David Edwards and John Roberts (Platform Porters), unknown (Outside Porter), ? Edge (Parcel Porter), William Murray (Parcel Clerk), Mrs W James (wife of Station Master), Miss James (daughter of Station Master), Miss Lunt (Refreshment Room), J Matthews (a Wrexhamite), Mr I Perrott (Goods Inspector), Mr C W Paget (District Agent), Mr William James (Station Master), Mr W H Barratt (Booking Clerk), Mr C W Tinsley (Book Stall).

16. National Eisteddfod, Wrexham 1876

The National Eisteddfod was held in Wrexham in 1876 with the Pavilion being erected in the grounds of Brynyffynnon House (where the new Island Green shopping precinct is being built). This is possibly the oldest surviving photograph of the interior of any Eisteddfod Pavilion. Of particular interest is the wooden semi-dome over the stage which was designed to improve the acoustics and the mirrors at the rear of the stage. The Bardic Chair can be clearly seen in the centre of the stage.

The negative from which this print was made was undoubtedly glass and the top left and top right areas (shown as blank grey areas in this print) were broken off.

17. National Eisteddfod, Wrexham 1876

A photograph of the Gorsedd and officials taken outside No1 Grosvenor Road. The Chaired Bard, Taliesin o Eifion, had died on the day that he had submitted his entry and, consequently, the Chair was draped with black cloth, a procedure which was repeated at the 1917 Eisteddfod in Birkenhead.

Back row: Dewi Wyn o Eslet ?; Tegerin; Owen Hughes; O Owen (Menai Bridge); Menai Wyson; Dr Williams (Chairman Executive Committee); Dr Eaton Jones; Hugh Davies (Hon Secretary); Dewi Ogwen; R Lloyd (ex-Mayor); Ioan Pedr; Y Gohebydd; James Sauvage; Mynorydd; Carwad; Idris Vychan.

Front row: Andreas o Vôn; Lloyd Jones; Nathan Dyfed; Gethin Jones; Tudno; Kate Wynne; Hwfa Môn; Gwalchmai; Edith Wynne; Ellis Wyn o Wyrfai; Iolo Trefaldwyn; Ceiriog; W Cadwaladr Davies; Tudur; Idrisyn.

19. (Above) General Election, 1880
A political cartoon lampooning the Conservative candidate, the Hon George T Kenyon who lost the Denbigh Boroughs election to the Liberal, Sir Robert A Cunliffe. The script reads: 'Hon G T Kenyon's Committee Room—An hour is allowed to drink to get up nerve enough to read the results of the canvass' and 'Vote for Hon G T Kenyon and you shall have Beer Bribery Bunkum & Beaconsfield'.

18. General Election, 1885
The Conservative candidate, Sir Watkin Williams Wynn, appears on the balcony of the Conservative Club in High Street (now the Cosmopolitan Wine Bar) to acknowledge the cheers of his supporters. Sir Watkin stood for the Denbigh East constituency and lost to the Liberal George Osborne Morgan.

20. Sir Evan Morris
A member of the Cambrian Leather Works family, Evan Morris was a solicitor with a practice in Temple Row (he later moved to The Priory). He served as Mayor in 1888 and, when Queen Victoria visited the town in August 1889, was knighted. He lived at Highfield—then Roseneath— and retired in 1890 when he moved to Eastbourne where he died aged 47.

Commemorative Medals

21 & 22. (Right) Royal Visit, 1889

The obverse shows the head of the Queen with the inscription: CROESAW I'W MAWRHYDI I GYMRU GU — CALON WRTH GALON. The reverse is inscribed: IN COMMEMORATION OF THE VISIT OF HER MOST GRACIOUS MAJESTY QUEEN VICTORIA TO NORTH WALES AUGUST 24TH 1889.

23. (Left) Royal Visit, 1889

The obverse shows the head of the Queen with the inscription: TO COMMEMORATE THE VISIT OF HM QUEEN VICTORIA TO WREXHAM AUGUST 24TH 1889. The reverse shows the Arms of the Borough of Wrexham with the inscription: PRESENTED TO OUR SUNDAY SCHOLARS MAJOR EVAN MORRIS MAYOR.

24 & 25. Victoria Board Schools, 1901

The British Schools had opened purpose built premises in Brook Street in 1844. In 1901, the local School Board built the Victoria Schools on Poyser Street which were opened in 1901 with Mr Charles Dodd as the first Headmaster. The old school building became the Victoria Hall and still survives as a night-club. This medal was issued to commemorate the opening of the Victoria Schools. On the obverse is a picture of the new schools with the inscription: 'IN COMMEMORATION OF THE OPENING OF THE VICTORIA BOARD SCHOOLS, WREXHAM JAN 1 1901' and on the reverse is a picture of the old Brook Street school with the inscription: 'BRITISH SCHOOL BUILT 1844. PRESENTED BY COUNCILLOR THOMAS JONES MAYOR OF WREXHAM'.

26. High Street, c1893

Many of the features seen in this photograph of High Street are still recognisable today. The second building on the left with its balcony just visible in front of the Provincial Insurance Company's building was the Conservative Club (see photograph 18). The Lion building on the extreme right had been one of the town's major hotels until the late 19th century and is seen here as the premises of S R Johnson, wine and spirit merchants; the site is now occupied by the Midland Bank. The Town Hall (built in the early 18th century) was demolished in the spring of 1940 as part of a road widening scheme.

27. The Old Vicarage, c1900

Located at the top of Vicarage Hill with the front door facing Abbot Street, this fine 18th century house appears on the 1748 print of Wrexham by S & N Buck. It was the parish Vicarage until the mid 19th century when the Rev Cunliffe moved into his own property at Llwyn Isaf (the site of the present Guildhall) and the old Vicarage was allowed to fall into disrepair. During the building of the Wrexham-Ellesmere railway line, this served as offices for the contractors and, at the time of this photograph, was the office of the Engineer of the Wrexham & Ellesmere Railway. The gable end of the railway booking office/waiting rooms for the Central Station can just be seen on the extreme right of this photograph with the water tower and platform canopy on the extreme left. The house was demolished shortly after this picture was taken. It was while visiting the old Vicarage that Reginald Heeber wrote his famous hymn 'From Greenland's Icy Mountains' which became an almost unofficial anthem for the British Empire.

28. Chester Street, c1890

A unique photograph showing the view along Chester Street from a spot close to the present-day RWF War Memorial. The trees on the left were in the grounds of Bodhyfryd House (the site of the present Crown Buildings). The wall on the right was the boundary of the grounds of Llwyn Isaf. The house in the foreground was the Chapel House for the Chester Street Baptist Chapel (which can be seen behind it) which was demolished to make way for the Chapel School Room which now houses the chapel itself. In the far distance the portico of The Old Registry building can just be made out.

29. Llwyn Isaf

In the 19th century this was the property of Rev George Cunliffe, vicar of Wrexham, and it was he that moved the vicarage here from the Old Vicarage (see photograph 27). In 1875, Rev Cunliffe gave it to the church for the use of his successors as vicar. It was purchased by the Council in 1953 for £6,436 and demolished to make way for the present Guildhall building.

30. Fire Brigade

The first official fire brigade in Wrexham was established by the Provincial Insurance Company of High Street and was taken over by The Prince of Wales' Volunteer Fire Brigade in about 1870. This was manned by local volunteers, mostly businessmen, and led by Captain Scott of the Seven Stars public house. In 1895, the Borough Council established its own fire brigade which was housed in a wing of the Guildhall in Chester Street. This small, horse-drawn engine was photographed in front of the Fire Station in Guildhall Square.

31. Prince of Wales' Volunteer Fire Brigade

A button, possibly the only item of the uniform of this public spirited organisation known to have survived. They wore dark uniforms with crested brass helmets.

32. Guildhall Square

The old Grammar School building (left) was purchased by Wrexham Borough Council in 1884. The extension in the centre of the photograph housed a Free Library which had previously been located in the Upper Assembly Room of the old Town Hall in High Street. The Fire Station was on the ground floor of the building on the right of the photograph (with a fireman standing in front of the public fire alarm).

33 & 34. Mr & Mrs Palmer

Alfred Neobard Palmer, a native of Norfolk, came to Wrexham to take up an appointment as industrial chemist to the Zodone Works in Pentrefelin. His driving passion was for local history and between 1893 and his death in 1915 he published numerous books and articles on the history of Wrexham and its neighbourhood. His wife, Esther, was the daughter of John Francis one of the leading figures in the Welsh community of Manchester. In 1894, Palmer went to live at Inglenook in Bersham Road and became a close friend of Edward Hughes.

35. (Below) Field Marshal Roberts Visit, 1903

In 1903, the last Commander-in-Chief of the British Army, Field Marshal Earl Roberts of Kandahar, VC, visited Wrexham to officially open the new Drill Hall in Poyser Street as the Headquarters of the 4th (Volunteer) Battalion, RWF. This photograph shows Lord Roberts inspecting the RWF Guard of Honour on his arrival at the GWR Station.

36. (Above) Civic Dignitaries, 1907

A unique photograph taken in September 1907 showing: Mr Thomas Bury, Mr J Allington Hughes, Mr John Bury and Mr Edward Hughes. Thomas Bury was the second Town Clerk of Wrexham (1879-1906) and the first person to be made a Freeman of the Borough. John Bury was the last surviving member of the first Town Council (elected in 1857 he came second in the poll with 324 votes). J Allington Hughes was the founder of the well known legal practice which still bears his name. Edward Hughes was in his second year of office as Mayor.

37. Plas Gwern

The only known surviving photograph of Plas Gwern which was demolished in 1888. A N Palmer wrote in his *History of the Town of Wrexham* (p155-7): 'The most important house in Tuttle Street was that which before the end of the seventeenth century was called Plas Gwern ... it stood at the back of the Nags Head in the premises of Messrs F W Soames and Company. I believe the very hill on which it was placed is now levelled. I have some reason for believing that Plas Gwern is the same house that ... was, in the time of Queen Elizabeth and King James I, called Y Bryn'. By the eighteenth century the house belonged to a Mr Davies who also owned the Nag's Head. When this photograph was taken, shortly before the house was demolished, it was obviously in a bad state of neglect and was being used as a barrel store for Soames' brewery.

38. Guildhall Square, 1905

To commemorate the reign of Queen Victoria (who died in 1901), Wrexham Borough Council placed a commission with Henry Price to produce a statue of the late Queen for siting in front of the Guildhall facing Chester Street. Price was a former student of the Wrexham College of Art and had been commissioned to produce a bronze statue of the Queen for the parade ground at Aldershot. The Wrexham statue was a duplicate of this and was unveiled on 1 May 1905. In later years the statue was moved to its present position in front of the Community Centre in Parciau.

39. Henry Price

In May 1905, on the occasion of the unveiling of the statue of Queen Victoria, the sculptor made a return visit to the Wrexham College of Art.

40. The Pentice, c1890

This property was located on Pen-y-bryn, between Tenters Square and Ruthin Road. The name Pentice is a corruption of Penthouse which was originally a description for a house with an upper storey that projected over the pavement. The plaque in the gable bore the initials T E W (which probably stood for Thomas Whitbread) and the date 1691. The house was demolished in about 1890.

41. The Highgate Inn

One of the oldest public houses in Wrexham, the Highgate Inn stood on Pen-y-bryn, opposite the junction of Chapel Street. Palmer found records dating from 1680 which refered to this property.

Royal Visit, 1903

On 8 May 1903, the Prince and Princess of Wales (later King George V and Queen Mary) visited Wrexham to unveil a memorial to the Officers, NCOs and Men of the Royal Welsh Fusiliers who had died in South Africa during the Boer War. Various photographs of this event have survived in the Glyndŵr Collection and they are of particular value in that they clearly show various Wrexham street scenes.

42. (Left) Members of the Denbighshire Hussars Imperial Yeomanry (left) and the Royal Welsh Fusiliers (with the Regimental Goat) await the arrival of the Royal party at the gates of Hightown Barracks.

43. (Below) A male voice choir performs before the Prince and Princess of Wales on the parade ground at Hightown Barracks.

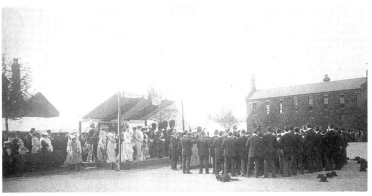

44. (Below) Members of Wrexham Borough Council make their way from High Street into Church Street to await the arrival of the Royal party. The streets are lined with men from the Royal Welsh Fusiliers. The corner building in the background is Dutton's 'Sigaro Stores'.

45. (Below) The Royal party proceeding along Regent Street. The escort and the men lining the pavements are provided by the Denbighshire Yeomanry. Note the tram rails set into the road surface.

46. (Above) The Royal party on Hope Street, approaching High Street. The men lining the pavements are provided by the Royal Welsh Fusiliers. The buildings on the left are on the site now occupied by the Littlewoods store.

48. (Below) The Prince (wearing the uniform of Colonel-in-Chief of the RWF) and Princess of Wales walk along Church Street to meet local civic dignitaries.

47. (Above) The Prince and Princess of Wales, escorted by the Denbighshire Yeomanry, travelling along High Street en route to the Parish Church.

49. The Royal party walking up Church Street after leaving the Parish Church. The mounted contingent of the Denbighshire Yeomanry are wearing the slouch hat style uniform popularised by the Boer War.

50. (Below) The Royal party in an open carriage proceeding up Acton Hill, past the main gates to Acton Hall.

51. Civic Procession, 1910
Members of Wrexham Council, proceeded by members of the town Fire Brigade, make their way along High Street to the Parish Church for the Memorial Service of King Edward VII.

52. Fairy Road, c1905

A steam roller emerges from Erddig Road into Fairy Road. This area of the town was laid out during the latter part of the 19th century when prominent local businessmen commissioned architects to design large villa style houses on the edge of the town, as close as possible to Erddig, the most notable country estate in the area. The first of these houses was Plas Tirion (now the home of the Roman Catholic Bishop of Wrexham) on Sontley Road.

53. Fairy Road, c1905

The junction of Fairy Road and Ruabon Road, seen from Victoria Road. The name Fairy Road is taken from the ancient burial mound (now located in the garden of one of the houses) which local legend declared to be a fairy mount.

54. (Left) General Election, 1906

Campaign publicity for A S Griffith-Boscawen who fought the Denbigh East constituency for the Conservatives in the 1906 General Election. He was defeated by the Liberal E G Hemmerde.

55. (Above) General Election, 1906

Campaign publicity, in the form of a railway ticket, for the Hon G T Kenyon, losing Conservative candidate in the 1906 General Election. Kenyon had held this seat at previous elections but in 1906 the Conservatives lost every seat in Wales.

56. Push Ball, 1907

A Push Ball match at the Racecourse ground, Wrexham on 30 August, 1907. The team in white shirts is made up of fireman from the Wrexham Borough Fire Brigade, with two officers in uniform on the right of the group. The presence of Edward Hughes on the left of the group would suggest that the team in dark shirts may have represented the Cambrian Leather Works.

57. Wrexham Corporation Jubilee, 1907

Back row: S E Allen (Borough Accountant); D Roberts (Market Superintendent); J W Jones (Cemetery Superintendent); J K Jones (Borough Collector); J England (Borough Engineer); W G Pickvance (Electrical Engineer); W J Fletcher (Veterinary Surgeon); C Heywood (Assistant Overseer). 3rd row: Deputy Chief Constable Edward Jones; J W Rogers (Deputy Town Clerk); Cllr P M Lewis; Cllr T Sauvage; Cllr F Sisson; Cllr S Edwards Jones; Cllr R W Glascodine; W L Wynne (Borough Treasurer); J Allington Hughes. 2nd row: J H Bate (Magistrates' Clerk); Cllr W J Williams; Cllr S G Jarman; Lawson Taylor (Town Clerk); C Moore (Sergeant-at-Mace); Dr D Ll Williams (Medical Officer of Health); Cllr J Stanford; Cllr Hugh Evans. *Front row:* Ald J B Francis; Ald R Williamson; Cllr E Birkett Evans (Ex Mayor); Cllr Edward Hughes (Mayor); Ald W E Samuel; Ald Thomas Jones; Cllr T B Taylor. Photograph taken outside the County Buildings.

58. National Eisteddfod Proclamation, 1911

Each National Eisteddfod is proclaimed twelve months before the event is held. Here, Members of Wrexham Council lead the procession for the Proclamation of the 1912 National Eisteddfod along Regent Street.

The corner of Duke Street can just be seen in the extreme bottom left hand corner of the photograph.

This picture was probably taken by James Dougal from the window of the Chicago Photographic Studio.

59. (Above) National Eisteddfod Proclamation, 1911

Members of the Boys Brigade, followed by the Borough Fire Brigade, parade through Hope Street en-route to the Proclamation Ceremony in Llwyn Isaf. In the background, the opening to the right of the Star Shop is Rainbow Passage.

60. (Below) National Eisteddfod Proclamation, 1911

Members of the Gorsedd walk in the procession along Hope Street, passing Phillips Tea merchants on the left (now Dollond & Aitchison).

61. National Eisteddfod Proclamation, 1911

Members of the Gorsedd of Bards gather in what appears to be the grounds of Llywn Isaf for the Proclamation of the 1912 National Eisteddfod of Wales.

62. (Below) National Eisteddfod Gorsedd, 1911

Members of the Gorsedd pose in front of the main door of Llwyn Isaf on the occasion of the Proclamation Ceremony of the 1912 National Eisteddfod of Wales.

63. Cambrian Leather Works, c1910
Staff of the Cambrian Leather Works, Salop Road (including Edward Hughes —who was Company Secretary—on the extreme left), pose beside stacks of treated skins.

64. Morgan Llwyd Memorial, 1912
Mrs Margaret Lloyd George (standing just to the right of the memorial), wife of the future Prime Minister, unveils the memorial to the Puritan divine Morgan Llwyd in Wrexham's Dissenters' Burial Ground, Rhosddu, 10 April 1912.

65. (Below) Mrs Margaret Lloyd George, 1912

A group photograph of leading non-conformist figures on the occasion of Mrs Margaret Lloyd George unveiling the Morgan Llwyd Memorial at the Dissenter's Burial Ground in Rhosddu (see photograph 64 opposite).

Front row: Mrs Ald Edward Hughes; Miss Gee (Denbigh); Mrs Ald Thomas Jones; Mrs John Owen (White House); Mrs Lloyd George (later Dame Margaret Lloyd George); Mrs Tom Ellis (widow of Tom Ellis, MP); Mrs E T John; Mrs W J Williams (Mayoress); Mrs Simon Jones.
Second row: Mrs J E Powell; Miss Calvin Thomas; Rev J Calvin Thomas; Ald Thomas Jones; Cllr W J Williams (Mayor); Sir Edward Anwyl; Mr E T John, MP; Mrs J S Lloyd; Miss Marion Owen (White House).
Back row: Ald Lewis Hughes (Amlwch); Mr J E Powell; Ald Edward Hughes; Mr Simon Jones; Rev R Peris Williams; Mr J S Lloyd. Photograph taken outside the Imperial Hotel.

Mrs Lloyd George was in Wrexham as her husband, then Chancellor of the Exchequer, was Day President at the National Eisteddfod.

66. Hafod-y-wern

This house, a large timber-framed building stood in roughly the same position as the present day Hafod-y-wern Primary School. According to Palmer, the first recorded resident of Hafod-y-wern was Hwfa ap Iorwerth who was alive during the mid-13th century. It passed in a direct line to his great-great grandson Hywel ap Goronwy and then, in the female line by marriage to John Puleston of Berse in the 15th century. Hafod-y-wern was by 1620 the principal free estate in the manor of Wrexham Regis. The house was, until 1829, approximately twice the size of the building that appears in this photograph but, at that time, the Great Hall (which would have stood to the left of the house in this photograph) and other rooms were demolished. In 1869, the house was let to Wrexham Borough as a sewage farm. Towards the end of the nineteenth century, the remaining wing of the old house was demolished and a new property was built on the same site.

67. Fund Raising

Members of the Hughes family and friends dressed in costumes for a Japanese Fair aimed at raising funds for the NSPCC. The photograph is taken outside the home of Dr Richard Evans.

68. (Below) Hughes Family

Mr & Mrs Edward Hughes, their three daughters (Gwendoline, Dorothy and Edna) and the family dog in the garden at Glyndŵr, Bersham Road.

69. (Right) Ar-y-bryn Terrace

Now demolished, this terrace faced Earl Street and backed on to Poplar Road. A N Palmer (see photograph 33) lived at No 3 for a number of years when he first moved to Wrexham in 1880.

70. Fire Brigade, 1914

The Corporation Fire Brigade acquired its first motorised fire engine (the first in north Wales), a Morris named *Maud Elsie,* in 1914 —an event deemed worthy of being recorded with an official photograph on Guildhall Square.

71. Frederic William Soames

The proprietor of F W Soames & Co, brewers in Mount Street (later the Border Brewery). He lived at Plas Fron, then Llwyn Onn and Plas Power before building a new house at Bryn Estyn (see photograph 72). He served as Mayor in 1891, 1901 and 1902.

72. Bryn Estyn Hall

This 20-bedroomed private house was built at the end of the 19th century by Mr F W Soames (see photograph 71 above) on the site of a previous house. Mrs Soames sold the house in 1928.

73. Peter Walker

The eldest son of Peter Walker, a Scotsman, who had settled in Liverpool where he had established a successful brewery. Peter (junior) and his brother Andrew joined their father in the family business. He trained as a brewer at the Cambrian Brewery in Wrexham before returning to Liverpool to run the expanding wine and spirit business owned by his father. From the 1840s, he resided at Coed-y-glyn, Wrexham although still involved with the family business. When his brother (later Sir Andrew Walker, founder of the Walker Art Gallery and the Walker Engineering Laboratories) took over the running of Walker's, Peter (junior) left and in 1860 took over a small brewery in Willow Road, Wrexham which he extended into one of the largest in the town. He served as Mayor from 1866-8 but felt slighted when he was turned down for a further term in office. He died at Coed-y-glyn on 13 April 1882, aged sixty-two and his brewery closed down the following year the business being transferred to Burton on Trent. He presented the Parish Church with its pulpit in 1867 and £1,000 was contributed towards the building of St Giles Schools, Madeira Hill. His name is recorded on the Salop Road Bridge (now known as the Willow Bridge) which he rebuilt at his own expense.

74. (Left) Joseph Clark

Born in Cumberland, he was a partner in the Clark & Orford Brewery which became the Cambrian Brewery. He lived at Pen-y-bryn House. Clark was Mayor in 1864, four years after his brother John had held the office, and presented the Corporation with its Silver Mace. He died in 1881.

75. (Right) John Beirne

Born in Ireland, Beirne established a successful chandlery and pawnbrokers business in Charles Street (the present day Bumbles shop) and a brewery below the Parish Church (in what is now the Albion car park). He lived at Plas Derwen and died in 1890.

Wrexham Co-operative Society Ltd, 1911

The Wrexham Co-operative Society was established in 1890 by the management and staff of the Cambrian Leather Works, with J Meredith Jones as President and Edward Hughes as Secretary. The first shop was opened in Abbot Street on 5 May 1890. Edward Hughes resigned as Secretary in May 1890 and his duties were taken over by Mr J G Crompton.

77. (Above) WCS stables, 1908.   79. (Below) Hightown store, 1909.

76. Wrexham Co-operative society Central Premises, 23 & 24 Abbot Street.

78. Rhosddu Road store, 1904.

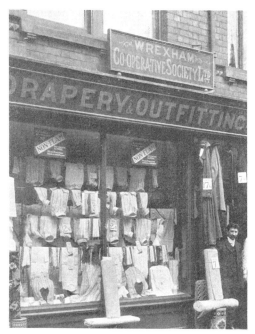

80. (Above) Bradley Road store and bakery, 1896.

81. (Left) Drapery store, 19b Abbot Street, 1911.

82. (Below) Interior of the 'Model Bakery' Bradley Road.

Denbighshire Volunteer Regiment

The ever increasing demands for men brought about by the expansion of the armed forces very soon after the outbreak of war in 1914 led to moves to form volunteer units to assist with home defence from those men unable to serve in the regular army due to age or the nature of their occupation. The concept was very similar to that of the Home Guard during the Second World War with units serving on a part-time basis.

83. (Left) By April 1915, the new volunteer defence force was in the process of being formed and meetings were to be held at Alexandra School on Tuesdays, Wednesdays, Fridays and Saturdays with route marches arranged for Sunday mornings. By November 1915, the Volunteer Training Corps had expanded sufficiently to form a regiment covering the old county of Denbighshire comprised of two battalions. The Eastern Battalion was centred on Wrexham with units in most of the surrounding towns and villages. By this time the force had expanded its role to 'provide opportunities of preliminary training for those men who enlist in the Regular Army'.

84. (Above) Edward Hughes was commissioned as a lieutenant in the new volunteer corps (Wrexham Unit) and was Quartermaster. Here the unit poses for a photograph during a period at camp (probably at Ilandrillo-yn-rhos). Edward Hughes is seated just right of centre wearing the darker uniform. The lighter uniform worn by the majority of the officers and men may have been a means of differentiating between the volunteer and the regular army units.

85. Croesnewydd Hospital, August 1916

During the First World War, Croesnewydd Hospital was taken over as a military hospital. Here a number of wounded servicemen (some wearing the normal army uniform and others wearing the 'Hospital Blues' uniform issued to patients), pose for a photograph with members of the nursing staff.

86. (Left) Conscription

The introduction of conscription in 1916 led to large numbers of potential soldiers claiming exemption from military service on a variety of grounds e.g. conscientious objection. In each area an Appeals Tribunal was set up to listen to the arguments being put forward. Edward Hughes was appointed to serve on the Wrexham Appeals Tribunal and, as a consequence, received a number of anonymous letters such as this cartoon questioning his actions.

87. (Right) Wrexham Recruiting Office Staff, September 1916

Included in this photograph (taken at the rear of the then Public Library) are: Mr Carrington, Captain Penry, Mr Seymour Jones, Mr Evans, Mr Crapper, Mr Cyril Jones.

88. Return of the RWF, 1919
The Band of the 1st Bn, Royal Welsh Fusiliers, leading the Colours as they march off Chester Street into Guildhall Square on Saturday 1 June, 1919, on the occasion of the regiment's return to the town prior to demobilisation.

89. (Right) Return of the RWF, 1919
The Deputy Mayor of Wrexham (Alderman Edward Hughes) addresses the men of the RWF on Guildhall Square, 1 June 1919.

90. (Left) RWF Memorial, 15 November 1924
The memorial to the 10,000 officers and men lost while serving with the Royal Welsh Fusiliers during the First World War was sculpted by Sir William Goscombe John, RA and shows an 18th century Fusilier passing the Colours into the hands of a Fusilier from the First World War. The memorial was originally sited on the corner of Regent Street and Grosvenor Road but was moved to its present site on Bodhyfryd as part of a road widening scheme. In this photograph, the memorial, shrouded by the Union Flag, is about to be unveiled by Lieutenant-General Sir Francis Lloyd, GCVO, KCB, DSO, Colonel of the Royal Welsh Fusiliers.

Oppenheimer's Diamond Factory, 1918

Mr Bernard Oppenheimer, a Belgian diamond merchant, opened a diamond polishing factory in Acton Park towards the end of the First World War. The workers of the factory were drawn from the ranks of the disabled servicemen.

Unfortunately, Oppenheimer died in 1921 and the factory closed shortly afterwards. By 1923, the building had been converted and opened as Acton Park School.

91. (Above left) The main entrance to the diamond factory. The Oppenheimer monogram and the date 1918 can be seen above the door.

92. (Above right) The main factory building (Ald Edward Hughes walking in the foreground).

93 & 94. Two interior views of the diamond factory.

95. Visit of Rt Hon David Lloyd George, 1923

The former Prime Minister, the Rt Hon David Lloyd George was granted the Freedom of the Borough of Wrexham in 1923. Included in the photograph are: *Front row:* Cllr T B Taylor; Miss Megan Lloyd George (later Lady Megan, MP for Anglesey and Carmarthen); Ald Edward Hughes; Mrs Cris Davies (Mayoress); Rt Hon David Lloyd George; Cllr Cris Davies (Mayor); Dame Margaret Lloyd George; unknown; Cllr W J Williams.

96. Acton Park Housing Estate, 1920

Planned by Sir Patrick Abercrombie in 1918, the Acton Park Estate was the first corporation housing development in Wrexham. Sixty acres of land along the north side of Rhosnesni Lane was bought from Mr Bernard Oppenheimer (a Belgian diamond merchant who had recently purchased 224 acres of land from Sir Neville Cunliffe — comprising the whole of the Acton Park Estate, including the Nine Acre Field alongside Rhosnesni Lane). The programme to build 118 houses at a cost of £100,000 commenced in 1923. This photograph, taken on 20 July that year, shows a commemorative plaque being laid in the wall of one of the first houses to be built. The Mayor at this time was Thomas Sauvage. It was intended that the original neo-Georgian style houses and crescents would form only a small part of the overall award-winning plan which was centred on Marsh Crescent and Neville Crescent.

97. Royal Visit, November 1923

Following his visit to Bangor to unveil the North Wales War Memorial, the Prince of Wales visited Wrexham on 2 November when he laid the foundation stone for the new Wrexham & East Denbighshire War Memorial Hospital. In this photograph, the Prince (wearing a bowler hat) appears before the citizens of Wrexham on the band stand in Parciau.

98. (Below) Royal Visit, November 1923

Another of the duties carried out by the Prince of Wales on his visit to Wrexham was to inspect the Girl Guides, Boy Scouts and Wolf Cubs paraded on the Guildhall Square. In this photograph, the Prince (wearing a bowler hat) is escorted across the Square by the Mayor, Cllr Cris Davies.

99. Opening of the War Memorial Hospital, 1926

The War Memorial Hospital was officially opened on 9 June 1926 by HRH Prince Henry (later Duke of Gloucester). Here the official party is about to leave 1 Grosvenor Road, en-route to the hospital.

Left foreground: C P Williams, MP; unknown; Mr Lawson Taylor (Town Clerk). *Right foreground:* Ald Robert Sauvage; James C Lee (Asst Town Clerk). *Standing on the top step:* Lord Kenyon; G Douglas Coe (Borough Electrical Engineer); Dr T P Edwards (Medical Officer of Health); J W Rogers (Borough Treasurer); Cllr Walter Welch; Cllr W Emyr Williams; Cllr R T D Macdermott; Cllr W H Thomas; extreme rear unknown; Cllr George T Davies (Mayor); Cllr Cris Davies; HRH Prince Henry; Ald W J Williams; Ald Sydney Jarman; Ivor A Stephenson (Sergeant-at-Mace/Sanitary Inspector); Ald Edward Hughes; Cllr T B Taylor; Cllr C E Hickman; unknown; unknown; unknown; unknown. The identities of the ladies on the right is not recorded.

100. National Eisteddfod, Proclamation Ceremony, 1932

The Gorsedd pose before the Grove Park School buildings on the occasion of the Proclamation in 1932 of the National Eisteddfod of 1933. The ceremony itself took place on the school fields (on the site now occupied by the Wrexham Divisional Police Headquarters) and the Eisteddfod was held at Parciau.

101. Wrexham Horse Market
Wrexham was, for many hundreds of years, a noted agricultural market town. One of the open-air markets was the horse market, built on Eagles' Meadow—to the rear of the premises on Yorke Street and Mount Street. This photograph, taken before the construction of the Ellesmere Railway in the 1890s, shows the view towards the south-west, looking towards the Willow Brewery which is just visible in the hazy distance.

102. Willow House
This large house was located on Salop Road, just south of the junction with Willow Road. Palmer believed that it was mentioned in early 17th century documents and records that it was also known as Pont Tuttle, a reference to the nearby bridge over the river Gwenfro. In the mid 19th century, a small brewery was established at the house which eventually, under the ownership of Peter Walker, developed into the Willow Brewery. The 1872 Ordnance Survey of Wrexham shows the property as being a public house using the name Bridge House. In its latter years, the house and its grounds formed part of the Corporation Depôt.

103. Five Fords Sewage Works, 1932

Borough officials pose to record the opening of the extension at Five Fords Sewage Works, Marchwiel. This photograph is significant in that it identifies a large number of the individuals who played a prominent role in the administration of the town during the early part of the 20th century.